ISBN 978-1-4710-1698-1

DEDICATION.

This book is dedicated with thanks to the following:

Chrissy, Hunter & Taylor, my awesome wife & kids.

'Sailor' Bob Adamson, the person who was kind enough to point me in this direction 20 years ago.

Cameron Reilly, Brisbane, Australia 2011.

INTRODUCTION.

Many people find themselves living lives filled with guilt, fear, anxiety, anger and regret. Happiness is either something that they experience only momentarily or something that they can't control. It is fleeting and hard to maintain. Something "good" will happen, which makes them happy for a while, but then the old negative feelings eventually return. They are scared of losing their job, losing a loved one, or scared of personal illness. They feel angry at things people have done to them or to others, angry at the actions of politicians and corporations, angry at their lot in life. They regret things they have done in the past which have caused hurt to themselves or to others. These feelings weigh upon them to an extent that they cannot shake. So they try to find temporary distractions from the negative feelings through shopping, television, food, alcohol, drugs and sexual conquest. These attempts at finding happiness never seem to provide any long-term solace and often bring with them new things to feel unhappy about.

Life becomes one big cycle of searching for

happiness and the eventual return of the fear, anger and guilt.

I'm telling you that it doesn't have to be like this.

Would you like to live your life without feelings of guilt, anxiety, fear, anger or regret?

Would you like to constantly feel like everything is perfect, peaceful and as it should be?

I would like to show you how to live like this. It's a system of thought I have been using for twenty years and it's never let me down. This system of thought is based on some basic scientific principles that everyone can understand and apply to their life.

It is very simple, quick to learn and easy to apply. You don't need any prior understanding of philosophy or science. You don't need to spend years learning any new skills or techniques. You don't need to change your diet or twist your body into painful positions.

You will be able to apply it as soon as you've finished reading this book. This book will be all you ever need to live a life of permanent serenity and contentment.

And you probably think I'm crazy for suggesting

that it is possible. But bear with me.

Imagine for a moment an actor making a major motion picture (think "Die Hard") who bumps his head in the middle of filming. This bump creates a form of amnesia where he forgets for a while that he's an actor. He forgets that he's on a set, surrounded by other actors and professional stunt-people. He suddenly believes he is in a genuinely dangerous situation. Someone appears to be shooting at him. Other people are fighting him. There are explosions, dramatic events, danger all around.

What would his response be? Fear? Terror? Anxiety?

Now imagine that the director of the film realises something is awry and brings the film to a halt. She approaches the actor to ask what is wrong. Quickly, she and the medical team realise that the actor is suffering from amnesia. They try to assure him that this isn't real - there is no danger, he is just an actor in a film. But the actor refuses to believe them. It all appears so real!

Well that's what I'm about to tell you in this book - that you are like an actor in a film and none of this is what it seems.

In your case, the writer of the film was the Big

Bang. The director is the Laws Of Physics. You are being "acted" by these mechanisms. You always have been, since the day you were born. You have no free will. In fact, it's absurd to think you have free will.

While this may all seem, on the surface, rather disturbing (a bit like the amnesiac actor in the film probably feels when being told the same thing), it can actually be a wonderful, liberating realisation and one that will possibly change your life in ways you cannot possibly imagine.

Just like our actor who eventually realises that he has no reason for concern or fear or anxiety, you will also learn that your life is under control and everything is as it should be.

According to the ancient Greek writer Pausanias, the aphorism "Know Thyself" was inscribed in the forecourt of the Temple of Apollo at Delphi. Exactly who it is attributed to is uncertain (possibly Pythagoras or Socrates).

Today, thanks to the discipline of science, we know more about ourselves and the universe that we live in than the author of the inscription could probably have ever imagined. If we are to truly know ourselves, if we are to know how to live, we must understand as much as possible about who - and what - we truly are.

In this book, we will examine three illusions pertaining to who we are - the illusion of free will, the illusion of identity and the illusion of time.

Dispelling these three illusions, these mistaken ideas, through the understanding of some basic scientific principles, will allow you to live your life with serenity.

Still think I'm nuts? That's fine. Just read the next chapter. It's pretty short. If, after that, you still think this it's nonsense, put the book down and go about your life. No hard feelings. Give me the next ten minutes of your life and if you're still not interested in learning more then we can part friends. Deal? Cool.

Let's get started.

THE ILLUSION OF FREE WILL.

If you can get your head around this chapter, then you'll already be 90% of the way to finding serenity. This is the key that unlocks the door to everything else.

It's probably going to be a little difficult to accept at first, but I ask you to suspend your disbelief until you've completely digested the concept I'm about to share with you.

Okay. Ready? Take a deep breath. Good.

This might shock you - but you don't have any free will. You never did and you never will. The idea of "free will" is completely unscientific. Understanding and accepting that fact will change your life.

Philosophers and scientists continue to debate about how much free will we have, even though there is zero evidence to support the theory and increasing scientific evidence to refute it. However, like the idea of gods, aliens and Elvis being still alive and hiding in Argentina, "free will" seems to be one of those ideas that people just find hard to let go of, regardless of a complete lack of evidence.

Negating the theory of free will is actually extremely simple and, once you've read this chapter, you'll be able to let go of it forever. I promise you'll be much better off as a result.

What Do We Mean By 'Free Will'?

Let's start with the definition of 'free will' because, as Plato said, "the definition of terms is the beginning of wisdom."

The common definition of 'free will' is that we have control over our thoughts and actions *outside of cause and effect*. The dictionary on my Mac defines free will as "the power of acting without the constraint of necessity or fate; the ability to act at one's own discretion". The common idea of free will is that you can think and act independently of what is happening in the universe around you; that you can tear yourself away from the forces of nature to act completely independently. We just hate to think that our lives are governed by external events. It would suggest that we are automatons, trapped in a completely clockwork world, destined for a fate not of our choosing. It's not a question about whether or not you have thoughts or if your brain makes decisions. It's a question of whether or not the thoughts and decisions you have are 100% governed by things outside of your control or not.

And it's not just external forces that we need to break free from in order to truly have free will - we also need to somehow break free of the *internal* forces - the chemical forces that govern the way our brains function.

I believe that this basic idea is the root of most of our emotional problems. It is so completely topsy-turvy to what is really going on, that it seriously screws people up. The only reason you probably haven't noticed this before is that you probably think you have free will too, so you're just as screwed up as the rest. Once you realise you don't have it, never did and never will, you'll be a lot better off.

This isn't to suggest that we don't have thoughts or that decisions aren't made. Thoughts are a natural by-product of our brains. The important thing to recognise is that our brains are organic machines which operate according to the laws of chemistry. We didn't design the machine -

evolution did - and we certainly aren't in control of it's output.

Human action comes in two forms - subconscious actions and conscious actions.

Subconscious actions are usually not associated with 'free will' because, by definition, we aren't aware of the processes that precede the actions. How, then, does this action occur, if we aren't in control of it? Some subconscious actions, like pulling your finger off a burning stove, aren't controlled directly by the brain but by the nervous system. How does the nervous system work? It functions according to the laws of chemistry. Chemical signals are transmitted from your nervous system to your muscles. The brain isn't required to intervene in the process. And most people don't have a problem accepting that.

Other kinds of actions, like slamming your foot on the brakes of a car to avoid an accident, also don't seem to be preceded by thought but are obviously controlled by the brain. The brain seems to perform certain functions that we are unaware of, that aren't observed by the conscious mind, yet which cause actions to occur. In the instant another car swerves in front of your own, there isn't time to think "wow I better slam my foot on the brake". It just happens. Somehow an instruction obviously makes it way from the brain to the foot - but we aren't aware of it until after the fact. What process allows this to happen? Again, it's chemistry. Certain behaviours have been encoded into your brain's neuronal architecture through conditioning or training. The training you have received to slam your foot on the brakes is (hopefully) so deeply ingrained that you don't need conscious thoughts to get involved.

These are just some examples of subconscious actions that most people will agree have nothing to do with 'free will'.

Conscious actions are different in that they are preceded by thoughts. We are aware of the thought process as it happens and, consequently, feel in control of the resulting action.

For example, the question "Should I eat another piece of cheesecake or not?" is something we might think when presented with a delicious creamy temptation. That question will typically kick-start a chain reaction of thoughts such as: "Well it does look delicious... and I did go to the gym today.... but if I eat that then I really can't afford the calories of spaghetti bolognese tonight, and I really want to eat that as well... so I better choose between the two... okay, let's say no to the cheesecake."

In these situations we feel like we are in control of the thoughts and actions. Why? Simply because we are aware of them.

My question is - where did the original thought - "Should I eat another piece of cheesecake or not?"- come from? How did it start?

In the above example, did I *choose* to think the very first thought, "Should I eat..."? Or did it just... appear? Did it happen as the result of some subconscious process, such as the one that makes me stamp my foot on the brake pedal? Or did I consciously *choose* to think that particular thought?

If you think the latter is true - that you deliberately chose to think the "Should I eat" thought - let me ask you: where did the thought "I will choose to think the 'Should I eat' thought" come from? Did you choose to think *that* preceding thought? Or did *it* just appear via some subconscious process?

After a little bit of analysis, most people will agree that, at some stage, the original thought just appears in our mind through some kind of subconscious, chemical process.

"Okay," you might be thinking, "perhaps that original thought just appeared in my mind. But I chose the rest of them, so my final action is still under my control."

Under investigation, however, you'll soon realise that it doesn't work that way.

Can I Choose Which Thought I Act Upon?

Some people get stuck on this part of the argument, so I will try to give it serious attention. Some of you will try to argue something along the lines of the following:

"Okay, so I understand that I may not be in control of the first thing that comes into my head, but I *can* organise my thoughts towards a goal."

Let's break this down and see if it's true.

These successive thoughts - did you create them deliberately? Or did they also just appear via some unseen process?

If you can accept that the first thought appears through an automatic chemical process, why would the successive thoughts be any different?

Did you think "I will now think this thought" before thinking each thought? Or did they somehow happen by themselves, through some kind of chemical chain reaction?

In order to argue that you are somehow in control of these successive thoughts, that you are somehow "organising" them, you will need to demonstrate *how* you create or organise each thought. You will need to be able to explain the process you go through in order to create or organise thoughts. Most people, when asked this question, will answer something like:

"I just *think* them."

Yes, you do just think them. But *how* do you do that? What part of your brain do you squeeze to think a new thought? How are you in control of the process? Can you explain it? Could you draw me a diagram?

Most people get stuck on that point. Why? It's because *they have no idea*. The brain is just doing its thing. However because we are aware of the thoughts, we say to ourselves "I did that". But if you can't explain *how* you did it, I suggest that you *aren't* really in control of it. It's happening *to* you, in the same way your heart pumps blood through your body and your stomach digests your food. Do you believe that you are in conscious control of every capillary in your body? Do you have to think "beat, heart, beat!" one hundred and twenty times a minute? No, of course you don't. These processes happen without your mental involvement. And why? Because they function according to the laws of chemistry.

Well the brain, like the rest of your body, *also* functions according to the laws of chemistry.

To argue that you are somehow forcing your brain to create or organise thoughts in a manner that subverts the laws of chemistry, you'd have to explain exactly *how* you do that. And if you can prove that you break the laws of chemistry with your brain, you'll probably be up for the Nobel Prize in Chemistry, I believe the prize is one million dollars, so it's worth the effort.

In my experience, the thoughts just appear, one after another. Never in my life have I thought "I will now think a thought" before a thought appears. I wouldn't even know which neurons to squeeze or how to squeeze them in order to generate the mysterious electro-chemical event that creates thoughts.

Thoughts just happen by themselves.

Have you ever seen a video of ping pong balls set on mouse traps? (If you haven't, there's a great one on YouTube (Google "Sciencenter Mousetrap Cascade"). Our brains seem to work in a similar fashion. One thought starts a chemical chain reaction of thoughts. What we think of as "organising our thoughts towards a goal" and "making a decision" is really just that chain reaction playing itself through. The first thought - an electro-chemical event - triggers a succession of electro-chemical events ('thoughts') which lead to a further electro-chemical event (the 'decision to act'). How can you possibly think you are in control of these events? Isn't a more viable explanation that these events just happen because of chemistry?

Believing we are somehow, unexplainably, in control of this thought process is vain egoism. It strikes me as similar to the idea certain people had one thousand years ago that humans were the centre of the universe. We like to tell ourselves that we are somehow special, that we stand alone in the universe. It's a fallacy that not only generates a false worldview, it also severely interferes with our ability to live our lives in harmony and peace.

If you find that you are still stuck with this idea that you have the mystical ability to control or organise your thoughts, I challenge you to write down how you do it and email it to me (my email address is on the last page of the book). However if you can't explain how you do it in detail, then I submit that you really don't have control and should give up on the false belief. You'll be a lot happier as a result.

Predicting Volition

Every year there seems to be more scientific evidence to support the idea that we don't have control over our thoughts.

There have been a series of interesting scientific experiments performed over the last thirty years that provide some neurological insights into the decision-making process.

In February 2011, three neuroscientists produced a report that claimed to have made amazing progress. Here's a summary of their findings:

We recorded the activity of 1019 neurons while twelve subjects performed self-initiated finger movement. We report progressive neuronal recruitment over ~1500 ms *before subjects report making the decision to move*. We observed progressive increase or decrease in neuronal firing rate, particularly in the supplementary motor area (SMA), as the reported time of decision was

approached. A population of 256 SMA neurons is sufficient to predict in single trials the impending decision to move with accuracy greater than 80% already 700 ms prior to subjects' awareness. Furthermore, we predict, with a precision of a few hundred ms, the actual time point of this voluntary decision to move. We implement a computational model whereby volition emerges once a change in internally generated firing rate of neuronal assemblies crosses a threshold. (Itzhak Fried, Roy Mukamel, Gabriel Kreiman, 2011, ""Internally Generated Preactivation of Single Neurons in Human Medial Frontal Cortex Predicts Volition")

Building on the ground-breaking work of Benjamin Libet, who in 1983 performed some of the first scientific experiments on volition, Fried, Mukamel and Kreiman connected up their subjects' brains to instruments that could detect the firing of neurones. They then asked their subjects to look at a digital clock and, whenever they were ready, to raise a finger. They were also asked to observe the time that they made the decision to move their finger. This time and the actual time they raised their finger was recorded by the researchers.

What the researchers discovered was that their subjects' brains starting firing rapidly up to 1500 milliseconds *before* they reported having made the conscious decision to move their finger. What this seems to indicate is that the process of making the decision happened *before the subjects were even aware of it.* If your brain is making decisions before you are aware of the process taking place, how can we truly claim to have free will?

If you answer "well I made it happen", then, again, I ask you to explain in detail exactly how you did that.

What About Bell's Theorem?

Our brains are extremely complex chemical machines. Like everything else in our bodies, such as our nervous system and our digestive system, the brain functions according to the laws of chemistry. Neurons are cells. Cells are made of molecules. Molecules are made of atoms. Atoms obey the laws of chemistry and physics. It's all governed by Cause and Effect.

"Aha," I hear some of you thinking, "what about quantum mechanics? The laws of quantum physics allow for uncertainty. Perhaps somewhere in that uncertainty we have the source of free will. What about the Bell's Theorem?"

Well.... not so fast.

Bell's Theorem is very important in quantum physics. It is essentially a response to the so-called "EPR Paradox" (or Einstein–Podolsky–Rosen paradox), which challenged the notion that we can never know both the position and momentum of a particle (something Einstein struggled to accept for the last fifty years of his life). The EPR paper argued that even quantum particles must display evidence of causality and that something was missing from the quantum mechanical models in use at the time.

However, the late physicist John Stewart Bell devised experiments ("Bell's Theorem") which have since proven that some quantum effects appear to travel faster than light and has lead to experimental proof of the non-causality of the quantum universe.

Some believers in free will try to argue that non-causality of quantum particles leaves room for volition. "Perhaps," they argue, "our brains operate in the quantum scale and, therefore, get around cause and effect."

Can you really claim to consciously *control* these quantum events? Do you have a hidden instruction manual for operating sub-atomic particles? If not, then I suggest that you *aren't* consciously in control of them and, therefore, would be hard pressed to use them to support an argument for free will. Even if quantum uncertainty is involved in how your brain works, it's pretty hard for you to claim to be in the driver's seat unless you can explain how you make it work.

The Simple Model

Here a simple model to explain where decisions come from:

1. Decisions are thoughts.

2. Thoughts are properties of the brain.

3. The brain is made of chemicals.

4. Chemicals always obey the laws of chemistry (i.e. 'cause and effect').

5. Ipso facto - 100% of your thoughts, decisions and actions are always determined by cause and effect.

What Does It All Mean?

What does all this mean for how you live your life?

If you have no genuine control over your thoughts and actions, how does this change how you live, day to day?

Well we have to start by realising that you have *never* had free will, so why would anything dramatically change? You'll continue to do whatever you have to do, based on the laws of chemistry, of cause and effect. Sometimes people have this idea that if you don't have free will, you'll never leave your bed again. You'll just lie there and stare at the ceiling.

Try it. See how long it lasts.

The same chemical processes that have driven your life up until this point will continue to drive your life after you stop believing in free will. A few centuries ago, some people believed that the earth was flat. That erroneous belief didn't stop the world from orbiting the sun. When people accepted the central role of the sun in our solar system, the earth didn't fall out of the sky. The same processes that always governed the orbit of the earth continued unabated. So, too, with free will. Your life will continue just fine when you stop pretending that you possess free will.

What will change, however, is that you might no longer feel as much guilt, anxiety, fear, anger or stress. Why? Because these emotions no longer makes any sense when divorced from the concept

of free will.

For example...

Let's say you've been feeling guilty over something you once did. Once you realise that you did the only thing you could possibly do, according to the chemical structure of your brain at the time, then you will stop feeling guilty about it. You did what you had to do. There was no other possibility. Feeling guilty over something you had no control over just doesn't make any sense. It isn't rational.

Let's say someone once did something that hurt you and you've been feeling angry towards them. Once you realise that they did the only possible thing they could do, based on the chemical structure of their brain at the time, then you will feel less angry towards them. They did what they had to do. There was no other possibility. Feeling angry over something that the other person had no control over just doesn't make any sense. *It isn't rational.*

Let's say there is something that might happen in the future that you've been feeling fear, anxiety or stress about. Once you realise that all things happen as a result of the laws of physics, that events will happen as they must, people will do what they have to do, including yourself, then you will find that the fear, anxiety or stress dissipates. Things happen as they must, according to the laws of physics. Feeling worried over something you have absolutely no control over just doesn't make any sense. *It simply isn't rational.*

When we stop believing in the illusion of free will, life becomes much simpler, easy, peaceful. It doesn't, however, stop in its tracks. We continue to act and live as we did before. We just do it knowing that every thought and decision we (and others) make are the only possible thoughts and decisions we (or they) can make at that particular point in time, based on the chemical structure of our (their) brains.

We then surf through life, accepting all things that happen as the only possible things that could happen. We allow life to just happen. From my personal experience, and the experience of friends who share the same philosophy, this outlook on life leads to genuine, lasting peace and a feeling of deep happiness.

Can You Really Live As If You Don't Have Free Will?

Sometimes, after I talk about free will with people, they tell me that while free will might be unscientific and an illusion, it is a 'necessary illusion'. They seem to think that we *need* to believe in or at least act like we believe in free will, or somehow the world would stop turning.

I can assure you from personal experience that this isn't the case.

I stopped believing in free will about twenty years ago. Since that time, I've completely accepted that my thoughts, decisions and actions are merely the laws of physics and chemistry playing out.

Let me stress again that I'm not suggesting thoughts, decisions and actions don't occur. All I'm suggesting is that *when* they occur, they are the product of cause and effect, of physics, and not something that you have any control of whatsoever.

Every thought, decision or action you've ever had or done was the only possible thing that you *could* have done at that particular point in time based on the neural architecture and chemical composition of your brain at the time.

So living without the concept of free will is very much like living as you are used to, with only one significant difference - ownership. When you stop believing in free will, it's a bit like stopping believing in God. The world still turns, the universe still functions - the only change is that you realise that it's the work of natural laws, not some imaginary being (in the case of free will, the imaginary being is YOU) pulling the strings.

What About Morality?

One last thing about free will. People seem to get hung up on this as well.

Morals.

If we don't have free will, does this mean we can just go around doing whatever we want? Can we murder, rape and plunder free of guilt?

Well, the truth is - you'll do whatever your chemistry makes you do.

And if your chemistry makes you do those things, then so be it. Nothing can be done about it.

However...

What this doesn't mean is that a society that doesn't believe in free will must collapse into complete chaos and anarchy.

A couple of hundred years ago, when people committed certain crimes, their actions were blamed on devils possessing their souls. These unfortunate individuals were often burned at the stake, hung by the neck or drowned in the river.

In our more enlightened times, we realised the stupidity of these ideas and completely (albeit slowly) changed our models for why people do the things that they do. We now understand that people who commit crimes such as murder or rape aren't possessed by evil demons, they are mentally ill.

We have completely changed our models for why people do the things they do.

And yet society survived!

Society will also survive letting go of the illusion of free will.

When someone is dangerous to society, we need to protect the rest of society from them - whether or not they have free will. It doesn't matter if a serial killer has free will or not. These days, when we catch a serial killer, they are proclaimed by psychiatrists to be mentally disturbed and we take steps to protect society from them and attempt to rehabilitate them.

So don't worry about morals. Morals will remain once the idea of free will is abandoned in the same way that morals survived the abandonment of devils.

THE ILLUSION OF TIME.

When it comes to the subject of time, we should not be surprised to learn that science reveals, once again, that our senses deceive us.

We tend to think of time as something that flows or unfolds, moment by moment. It seems to us that the future hasn't happened yet and that the past is long gone.

Science, however, tell us something completely different.

Einstein was the first to realise that time and space are actually the same construct - therefore we now refer to it as "spacetime". Time is really just another dimension that we add to the three dimensions of space. Spacetime therefore has four dimensions: height, width, length - and time. The physics behind it is a little complicated (and I'm quite certain I don't fully understand it), but essentially Einstein demonstrated (and subsequent experiments have extensively confirmed) that time exists as a dimension of space. If all of space exists "now", then all of time also exists "now".

Einstein once wrote to the wife of a recently departed friend, "For we convinced physicists, the distinction between past, present, and future is only an illusion, however persistent."

Therefore, we need to think about time not as something that flows but as something that already exists - past, present and future - just like space.

It might help to think of spacetime as a very large box. All of space and time exists inside that box. It's simple enough for us to conceptualise the three spatial dimensions of the box - height, width and length. Time is just another dimension to add, one that is slightly harder for us to conceptualise because of how we experience it. We know however from physics that all of time exists fully formed inside that box. We move through time the same way we move through space. The trick is in realising that just because we haven't moved through a particular point in time yet doesn't mean that it doesn't already exist. In the same way that the space in a distant corner of the box exists even when we aren't in that corner, the time dimension of that part of the box also exists.

Imagine a room in your home. Imagine that you are standing in one corner of the room and a friend is standing in the opposite corner. We already understand that you each have a different location in space. What isn't as obvious is that you also occupy a different location in time. Even though your respective locations in time are infinitesimally minute, they are nonetheless distinct.

As a result, you both experience "now" differently.

Let's imagine you set up a simple experiment with your friend in the opposite corner.

You say to your friend "When I say the word 'now', raise your hand."

A few seconds later, you say "Now!" and your friend raises her hand.

It seems to both of you that you experience the same "now" moment.

If we were to study it in a laboratory, however, we would notice that it isn't so simple.

First of all, when you speak the word "now", it takes a fraction of a second for the sound waves to reach your friend's ears and for her brain to process what she's heard. It also takes a fraction of a second for her muscles to respond to her brain's command to raise her hand.

So the actual moment in time that you say "now"

and the moment she hears "now", are different moments.

This means that by the time she has heard you say "now", the moment is actually in your past and you have moved on into your future. You and your friend, while standing only a few metres apart, actually experience the "now" in different times.

And yet you co-exist. Her 'now' is your past. Your 'now' is in her future. And, of course, the opposite is also true. If she said "now" and you raised your hand, the same experiment would be reversed. Her 'now' moment would be in your future. The past, the future, and the present all seem to co-exist.

Everything that has ever happened - and everything that ever will happen - is happening right now.

Here's how theoretical physicist Brian Greene explains it in his excellent book "The Fabric Of The Cosmos":

In this way of thinking, events, regardless of when they happen from any particular perspective, just are. They all exist. They eternally occupy their particular point in spacetime. There is no flow. If you were having a great time at the stroke of midnight on New Year's Eve, 1999, you still are, since that is just one immutable location in

spacetime. It is tough to accept this description, since our worldview so forcefully distinguishes between past, present, and future. But if we stare intently at this familiar temporal scheme and confront it with the cold hard facts of modern physics, its only place of refuge seems to lie within the human mind.

Living In The Now

If the future co-exists with the present, you can stop worrying about it - because it's already happening. Right now. What would be the point of worrying about something that has already happened? It would be foolish, right? The rational response would be to accept that it has already happened and just to deal with it.

Worried about what might happen to your job? Well stop! It's already happened.

Worried about your health? Don't! Anything that might happen has already happened.

Worried about failure? Forget about it! You're life has already happened. You're just catching up to it.

Worried that your partner might be having an

affair? Stop it! If it's going to happen, it's already happening. Just accept it and do what you must.

When you learn to accept the true nature of time, you might find that you cease worrying about future events and instead learn to happily embrace them. That has certainly been my experience. What would be the point of worrying about things that you have no control over and that ultimately have to happen anyway?

Learning to happily embrace the fact that everything, all possible future events, has already happened is one of the keys to experiencing permanent serenity.

"But but but....", you ask, "how do I carry on my life when time seems to continue flowing?"

Good question.

Imagine always living in the present moment, in the 'Now' moment. It's very possible. It's how many of us live. We know that projecting about the future is pointless so we stop doing it. Not only is there absolutely no way to know what is going to happen in the future, it's already happened, so what's the point of conceptualising it? You're probably going to get it wrong anyway. It's a waste of energy. Why not reserve your energy for dealing with things when and how they occur?

The most wonderful part of this new paradigm is that living in the present moment, not worrying about the future or the past, is actually a much more enjoyable way to live. I think of it as surfing through life, riding the waves, not being concerned about where they are taking you, knowing fundamentally that they will take you where they *have* to take you. So, as they say, enjoy the journey and stop worrying about the destination.

Whatever happens *has* to happen exactly the way it does.

You might think of it like a TV show. The TV show of your life has already been written, cast, filmed, and edited. You're just catching up to what's happened. Each day is a new episode. Your role is to provide the laugh track!

If you find the idea that your life has already happened distasteful and hard to swallow, then you're probably not alone. Many of us have had it beaten into our brains that we are responsible for our actions and that our success or failure in life is completely determined by us. Countless self-help books have been written on the subject and thousands of motivational speakers charge exorbitant amounts of money to prance around on stage telling people that they can change their lives - all they have to do is take control! And then the people wonder why things just get worse. Perhaps it's because they are being told to swim in the wrong direction?

Everything that ever will happen, already has happened. Let me quote Einstein again: "For we convinced physicists, the distinction between past, present, and future is only an illusion, however persistent."

Accepting this and living with it is not only surprisingly easy, it is also liberating. It doesn't take away from the excitement and enjoyment of life at all. If anything, it enhances both things. Once we accept that our life is already pre-destined (not by any god but by the laws of physics), we can settle into the enjoyment of watching it unfold before us. When you stop worrying about and fighting the process, life becomes simple, stress-free, and peaceful.

If this seems like a philosophy you might expect to hear from a Bronze age religion ("Thy will, Lord, not mine"), that's probably not by accident. It seems that whether or not you ascribe the force of destiny to a mythical god or to the laws of physics, the outcome is the same. It's a recipe for peace with the world around you.

Friedrich Nietzsche, in his last original book "Ecce Homo", referred to this philosophy as "amor fati", the love of (one's) fate:

My formula for greatness in a human being is amor fati: that one wants nothing to be different, not forward, not backward, not in all eternity. Not merely bear what is necessary, still less conceal it--all idealism is mendaciousness in the face of what is necessary--but love it.

THE ILLUSION OF IDENTITY.

The final point in our journey of knowing ourselves is working out who - or what - we really are.

If I were to ask you "what are you?", you would probably answer "a person". If you're like most people, you probably think of yourself as a mind and a body. You might even think you have other bits as well, ill-defined concepts such as a 'spirit' or a 'soul'. I've never met anyone who can explain what those things actually are in any detail but they nonetheless remain part of many people's concepts of their identity. Some might use terms like "energy" as part of their definition, but again, that tends to be a loose, fluffy term. Ask them what, exactly, this energy is, and they are likely to quickly clam up. It's an idea that sounds spiritual and enlightened but it's rarely supported with any hard thinking.

Whatever your concept of what you are might be - that you are a person with a body, mind, soul or spirit - it is likely to be one of the reasons you aren't happy. Think about it - if you have the wrong idea about what something is, you won't know how to work it properly. For example, let's say you think a laptop computer is a coffee machine. You aren't going to have much success with it. You might spend your entire life trying to get the laptop to pull you a shot of espresso and you'd end up extremely frustrated (and with a broken laptop to boot).

This is also true with our lives. If you think one thing is going on, when in fact something else is going on, you're going to come away continually frustrated and disappointed with life.

Most of us spend our lives trying to force what we really are - a square peg - into what we *think* we are - something that should fit into a round hole.

This fundamental mistake is the cause of much unhappiness.

It is quite possible that you accept your definition about yourself - e.g. that you are a body, a mind, a soul, a spirit - as a *prima facie* truth. It is such a deep part of your psyche that you have never questioned it. Questioning the veracity of this definition would seem to be as ridiculous as questioning whether or not the sky is blue...

.... Until you realise that you learned in school that

the sky *isn't* really blue at all, that the blueness is an illusion. So perhaps it is possible that our definition of what we are is also an illusion that we have been operating under from the time we were a small child?

In order to find lasting happiness, we need to be willing to question our most basic concepts about ourselves. This is what the great mathematician and philosopher Rene Descartes realized when he declared "Cogito Ergo Sum" or "I Think Therefore I Am". He realised that everything else might be an illusion. The only thing he could be sure of - the only thing that he knew, for sure, existed - was the thinking. "I am thinking, therefore I must exist in some form."

Like Descartes, we should start there as well.

Let's start by examining the idea that we are the mind.

Stopping The Chattering Monkey

First of all, what is "the mind"? What exactly are we referring to when we say "the mind"? Is it an object that we can touch or see? Where is your "mind"?

It seems to me that when we say "mind", we are

actually referring to a constant stream of thoughts. What is the mind without thoughts? We use the term "mindless" to describe someone who doesn't think before they act. We describe someone who *does* think about their actions as being "mindful".

"Mind" is actually a collective term for the thoughts that buzz constantly through our... mind? Hold on. Is the mind instead the *container* of the thoughts? I had a thought. Where? In my mind. That seems confusing. Perhaps "mind" is also a synonym for "brain"?

This would make sense. "Mind" then becomes both the container of the thoughts (the brain) and the thoughts themselves, which are a by-product of the brain.

According to Wikipedia:

"The original meaning of Old English *gemynd* was the faculty of memory, not of thought in general. Hence *call to mind*, *come to mind*, *keep in mind*, *to have mind of*, etc. Old English had other words to express "mind", such as *hyge* "mind, spirit"."

Sometimes our language can get in the way of clarity.

When referring to our own minds, we usually refer

to it as "my" mind (for example, "I changed *my* mind"), because we have been taught that we are the owner of, and are in control of, the mind. Of course, the only tool we could possibly have to control the mind *is* the mind - which once again gets confusing. When I say "I changed my mind", I am actually saying that my mind changed itself. How does that work?

If Part A of the mind is controlling Part B of the mind, what is controlling Part A of the mind? Part C? This idea that we are in control of the mind is quite easy to challenge. For example, can you make it stop? Can you stop your mind from thinking new thoughts? I bet you've never even tried. Get a stopwatch or a clock with a second hand and try to stop all thoughts from appearing for 60 seconds. Can you do it? You're not even allowed to think "I don't have any thoughts". Or "wow that second hand is moving really slowly". Can you stop all thoughts? If not... why not? If you're in control of your thoughts, shouldn't you be able to stop them? Right?

Old Zen masters sometimes referred to the mind as the "chattering monkey" for this reason. It constantly chatters away over there in the corner and there's little we can do to stop it. As we saw in the first chapter, we really aren't in control of the mind at all. It functions purely according to the law of chemistry.

Our journey of understanding the mind has come a long way.

Ancient Egyptians apparently considered the brain worthless, believing the heart contained the soul and the mind, which is why we still say you should 'learn things by heart'.

About 2000 years later, the Ancient Greeks were the first to believe that consciousness arose in the brain. Hippocrates said, "It is the brain that is the messenger to the understanding [and] the brain interprets the understanding."

Modern neuroscience, of course, confirms that the mind is a function of the brain. Neuroscientists regularly use huge machines called fMRI ("functional magnetic resonance imaging") scanners to observe the way people's brains fire signals while they are thinking. While some hardline doubters might still object that observing one thing happen while another thing happens isn't proof of causality (i.e. correlation does not imply causation), very few neuroscientists disagree that thoughts ("the mind") are properties of the brain. Thoughts are part of what the brain does. Thinking might turn out to be a standard output of any sufficiently advanced computational system, but we'll leave that to the Artificial Intelligence researchers.

Thoughts are properties of the brain. Change the chemical structure of the brain, either through removing some of it in an operation or accident or by taking sufficient quantities of mind-altering drugs, and the thoughts that the brain produces change or disappear altogether (as in cases of amnesia or trauma).

So, if the mind is a property of the brain, which is itself part of the body, instead of saying "I'm a mind and a body" we can just say we are a body. The mind is merely a function of the body.

A City Called You

Your body is made of trillions of living organisms called cells. What you refer to as 'me' is not just one living organism, it's roughly 100 trillion organisms living in symbiosis. You're a colony of organisms, like a hive or a fungus. You are not a single unit - you are an army. You are a city. Millions of individual units of 'you' are being born and dying off every day.

So which group of these cells defines 'you'? The

group of cells that were alive last week? Or the group of cells that is alive today?

According to researchers at the 108th General Meeting of the American Society for Microbiology in Boston, the number of bacteria living within the body of the average healthy adult human are estimated to outnumber human cells 10 to 1. You might think "I am the body" but when only 10% of the cells in the body are actually even human cells.... what does that mean for your identity?

Let's think about all these cells for a minute (human and non-human).

These organisms are themselves made of molecules.

The molecules are made of atoms.

The atoms are made of electrons, protons and neutrons but are mostly.... space.

For example, a hydrogen atom is only about a ten millionth of a millimetre in diameter, but the proton in the middle is a hundred thousand times smaller, and the electron whizzing around the outside is *a thousand times smaller* than that. The rest of the atom is simply empty.

Imagine an atom blown up to the size of a football

stadium. The football sitting in the middle of the field is the proton. The electron is the relative size of sesame seed (although of course as an energy wave it's really not like a seed at all) appearing somewhere near the stadium fence. The rest of it is empty space.

Your body is made up of cells, which are made up of atoms, which are mostly empty space.

This might be what the old gurus meant when they said that we are 'illusions'. We only see what our senses tell us is there. Unfortunately, our senses don't tell us the full story. It's like looking at a television screen for the first time and thinking the people on it are real. If you get up closer to the screen you'll notice that they are just coloured dots. So which are they? Real people or just dots? They seem real enough. They appear to experience lives, laugh, cry, tremble. And they can make *you* laugh and cry and tremble. But are they real or not?

The exact same questions can be asked of you. Are you a real person or just a collection of atoms?

In both cases, can we say the person is merely a concept that we can believe in or not? I know when I'm watching a great TV show (such as "Mad Men") that I can get caught up in the stories of the characters, feel their joy, their pain and their grief. My wife and I will talk about their characters the next day, wonder what they will do next. We don't for a second, though, think that these character have any true reality. We know without having to think about it that they are merely actors playing a role and that our perception of them is merely coloured dots on a screen.

The same is true when I think about myself and my wife. I know that we appear to be independent entities, each with our own on-going story arcs, but I also know that this can't possibly be true. We, too, are just coloured dots (atoms) appearing on a screen (my mind).

Just as the cells in your body are 'born' and 'die', the atoms that make up your body come and go constantly. Every second of your life you are shedding atoms and attracting new ones. The food you eat and the air you breathe provide a constant flow of new atoms that become part of your body. In fact, studies have shown that 98 percent of the atoms in the body are replaced every year. (http://ti.me/yxkArP)

If you are 98% totally new atoms year after year... which group of atoms is the real you? This year's atoms or last year's? What about the atoms that will make up your body next year? Do you have any claim to them yet as being 'you'? As you can see, the concept of "me" is very flaky once we start to scratch the surface. And yet most of us take it for granted our entire lives.

That's Not My Left Arm

David Weisman, M.D., a neurologist in Pennsylvania, has done some interesting research involving people who have suffered from strokes to one side of their brain. Weisman recounts his experience with people who have suffered a stroke on the left side of their brain who then believe their left arm doesn't belong to them - they believe the arm belongs to the doctor, even though they are shown that is connected to their own body. When the patient's brain is experiencing trauma, it "comes up with something called a confabulation, creating a verbal fabrication to explain missing information. In this case the confabulation becomes, "That is your arm." Although nonsense and easy to falsify, the idea is internally consistent, makes some sense of the (messed up) internal data, and feels right. The injured brain creates a confabulation to maintain unity of self and a feeling of control."

In a recent edition of Psychology Today, he writes:

Our brain creates an illusion of unity and control where there really isn't any. There are thousands of cases and experiments that demonstrate why science supports a view of the unified mind as illusion rather than reality.

Yet again we see that our idea of who and what we are is easily confused. Our sense of identity, of being a single person instead of an army of cells and atoms, is a "confabulation" - a fabrication we invent to simplify our explanation of who and what we are.

What I have learned is that this confabulation complicates our lives extraordinarily. Once we dispose of it and accept the fact that our identity is much more complex, life becomes much simpler and peace is easier to maintain.

How Old Are You?

We have already seen that 98% of the atoms that make up our bodies were not part of our bodies a year ago. The question of how old you are is even weirder than that.

The human body is roughly made up of:

- 63% hydrogen;
- 24% oxygen;
- 12% carbon.

Most of the hydrogen is about 13.7 billion years old - it was formed in the Big Bang.

The oxygen and carbon are around 4.6 or 4.7 billion years old, being the remnants of one or more supernovae (i.e. exploding suns) that occurred just before our Sun itself formed.

So... how old are you?

If you date your age from when the current version of your body was made, you're about a year old.

But if you date yourself from when your components were themselves made, then the atoms that make up your body are somewhere between 4.6 and 13.7 billion years old. Let's take an average of 9 billion years.

So if you are 9 billion years old, why would you be worried about what might happen next week?

Probability Waves

The truth is that you do, of course, exist. It's logically impossible for something that doesn't exist to state "I do not exist". Something must exist in order for you to be reading this. The important question isn't really whether or not you exist. The important question is "what exists?" What is this thing that you are?

Are you a single homogenous entity known as a human being?

Or are you a colony of ever-changing living organisms?

Or are you a temporary configuration of frenetic atomic motion?

The atoms that were part of your body a year ago but aren't part of body today - are they still "you"? When do they stop becoming you? If atoms that once formed part of your body configuration are now part of something else in the universe - are you that thing also? Are you spread all over the place? If the atoms that currently make up your body were once part of an animal, a plant, a rock, another person and a star - you are all of those as well?

If you lost a finger in an accident and it was sitting in a freezer somewhere waiting to be stitched back on, would you consider it still part of you?

If so, why not have that level of attachment to the

atoms that were once part of you but are now part of something else (living or non-living)?

Just because we can't see them, should it mean they are any less important to our sense of identity?

But wait - it gets weirder.

One of the strangest aspects of quantum physics is the discovery that all sub-atomic particles - in other words, the things that make up all atoms, including protons, neutrons, electrons as well as photons, the particles of light - don't have a fixed position in spacetime until they are observed. As bizarre as this sounds and as contradictory as it seems to our everyday experience, an enormous series of experiments completed over the last 50 years have confirmed it to be undeniable. Until they are observed, all of these particles exist only as 'probability wave' - in other words, they don't actually exist anywhere in particular - they only have a probability of occurrence. This is known as "wave–particle duality". Current scientific theory holds that all particles exist only as a probability until they are observed. Nothing is real until it has been observed!

This isn't some kind of philosophical framework - physicists have confirmed this aspect of all matter experimentally, time and time again. It isn't just some mathematical framework or conceptual construct. Physicists actually conclude that every particle in the entire universe exists only as a wave function until it interacts with another particle, at which time it momentarily adopts a fixed position in space and time.

If you think this doesn't make any sense, you're in good company. Albert Einstein himself argued against this idea for the last 30 years of his life. He tried, again and again, to refute the science of probability waves and was determined to prove that quantum mechanics was a half-baked framework.

He failed.

And in the 50 years since his death, quantum mechanics has gone from strength to strength. So much so that only a small minority of physicists today disagree with the theory of the probability wave.

Physicists tell us that the electrons that orbit an atom's nucleus are really only a probability wave until observed, at which time they momentarily lock into a particular position or velocity (depending on which we're trying to measure - we can never know both at the same time, this being the idea behind Heisenberg's Uncertainty

Principle), before collapsing back into being a probability wave again. Electrons don't orbit around a nucleus like our Earth does the Sun (although that's the common school textbook conception). They are "smeared" across space-time, existing every-WHERE and every-WHEN - until observed. Although the electron as a higher probability of appearing in a certain location, it is theoretically possible for it to exist anywhere. Therefore, it must simultaneously exist everywhere.

This is true of all matter, including atoms and molecules, not just electrons.

So what does all this mean for who or what you are?

If the sub-atomic particles that make up your body are just a probability wave until observed, does this mean that you are a vague smear across space-time?

Is the entire universe just one big wave of matter?

That seems to be the position of some scientists.

Theoretical physicist Mendel Sachs, in his book "Quantum Mechanics and Gravity", suggests that there is only one universal wave. He wrote:

"Instead, one has a single, holistic continuum,

wherein what were formerly called discrete, separable particles of matter are instead the infinite number of distinguishable, though correlated manifestations of this continuum, that in principle is the universe."

This "single, holistic continuum" sounds remarkably like "the One" that is often spoken about by gurus and ancient philosophers such as Plotinus and Porphyry.

If the entire universe is a "single, holistic continuum", where do "you" start and finish?

Carver A. Mead, Professor Emeritus of Engineering and Applied Science at the California Institute of Technology (and, incidentally, the person credited with coining the term "Moore's Law"), also suggests in his book "Collective Electrodynamics: Quantum Foundations of Electromagnetism" that atoms are not particles at all but pure waves of matter. He writes:

"The quantum world is a world of waves, not particles. So we have to think of electron waves and proton waves and so on."

Look down at your body.

The atoms that make up your skin and hair aren't like miniature eggs with a hard shell. They have a fuzzy border, more like a cloud or a galaxy.

So where do "you" stop? And where does the chair you are sitting on start? Do the atoms that make up "you" and the atoms that make up the chair intermingle? If your eyes were powerful enough to see down to the atomic level, would it look like your atoms and the chair atoms blend into one another?

Okay, maybe you're thinking to yourself, "yes, but when I stand up, only some of the atoms come with me, those are the atoms that make me who I am". However, as we've already discovered, the atoms in "your" body come and go constantly, 98% of them being replaced every year. Are you defined by the 100 trillion atoms that happen to make up your body at any given time?

If you are 40 years old, your body consists of about 100 trillion atoms, and 98% of those atoms are replaced every year, that means that there are 3,920 trillion atoms out in the world somewhere that used to be part of you.

What level of identification do you have with them?

The late American physicist Richard Feynman once said:

So what is this mind of ours: what are these atoms with consciousness? Last week's potatoes! They now can remember what was going on in my mind a year ago -- a mind which has long ago been replaced. To note that the thing I call my individuality is only a pattern or dance, that is what it means when one discovers how long it takes for the atoms of my brain to be replaced by other atoms.

A pattern. A dance. In Indian religions, there is a term "maya". It is usually translated as meaning "illusion". Indian gurus often refer to the universe that we perceive as being "the dance of maya".

That's all you are. A pattern defined by a molecule called deoxyribonucleic acid (DNA). A pattern is information. A blueprint. A recipe. And a pattern is never the thing itself. You could eat a recipe for chocolate cake but it wouldn't taste anything like an actual chocolate cake. A blueprint for a jumbo jet won't fly you anywhere. A pattern isn't the thing itself, it's just a description.

So if you are just a pattern.... what does this mean for who or what you are?

Has your sense of identity started to fracture yet?

Let us first review what we've learned.

1. You exist, but not as a single unit.

2. The mind is a function of the brain and the body.

3. Your body is a colony of living organisms that die and are replaced constantly.

4. The body is also made of atoms, 98% of which are replaced every year.

5. Atoms are made up of sub-atomic particles that exist only as probability waves until observed, at which point they temporarily occupy a certain place in space-time, only to collapse back into being merely a probability wave again.

This leads me to the conclusion that "what I am" is something that's constantly in flux; impossible to define as "this" or "that". If sub-atomic particles are "probability waves" that are smeared across space-time, and I am made of those sub-atomic particles, then "what I am" must also be smeared across space-time, existing every-WHERE and every-WHEN.

I appear to be a body-mind. But the mind is only the body. The body is made up of cells. Cells are made of molecules. Molecules are made of atoms. And atoms are made mostly of space, the rest being spread out across space-time.

It's incredibly difficult to worry about what's happening at work or in your personal life when you remind yourself that what you really are is nothing more than a probability wave.

"Okay," I hear you thinking, "that's all well and good and probably scientifically accurate, but I still feel like me. How does this help me?"

It will only help you if you are prepared to let go of the illusion that you are something that you are not.

Plato, writing nearly 2500 years ago, used the analogy of people who spent their entire lives inside a cave, heads locked into a position so they could only stare forwards at a wall, with a large fire behind them that casts shadows on the wall. He said that if you told these people that the shadows weren't real, that there was something else, a deeper truth, they would think you were insane.

Illusions can be hard to let go of, especially when

they concern our identity and ego.

Imagine someone who has spent their lives inside a cinema, head locked in place, facing the screen. She has never seen another human being, only the people on the screen, who laugh, cry, exult, talk to her, and die. Then, one day, someone on the screen talks to her and says "Hey, guess what? I'm not real. I'm just lights being projected on a screen."

Of course, she wouldn't believe them. She would, at first, laugh the suggestion off, then argue that it wasn't rational, then probably get angry, then go into denial.

But then, if we let her out of her chair, and she walked up to the screen and looked very closely, she would see that they are, in fact, just lights, red, blue and yellow lights, flickering really fast. In fact, when she got up close to the screen, the people would all disappear. All she would see are lights.

If she walks back to her seat, the people coalesce again. But wouldn't the illusion be shattered forever?

Of course, we know that the people on the movie screen aren't really there, that they are just illusions. And yet we still cry, laugh, and scream at the movies. Why? If we know it's all an illusion, why do we still get emotionally involved?

Because that's what it's all about. That's why we go to the movies in the first place. To get emotionally involved in the story.

And that remains true for those us who realise the world at large is also an illusion. We remain emotionally involved in the story. Why? Because that's the whole point. That is our function.

However, when you leave the cinema, you cease worrying about the characters. You let them go. You know, deep down, that it was all an illusion. You don't lie awake at night worrying about what's going to happen to Iron Man tomorrow.

And those of us who realise the world is an illusion are able to let go of the characters in it in the same way. We can be emotionally involved but we can also let go and accept that it's all an illusion. We can sit in the seat and see the characters, but, like the girl in the cinema, we've been up close and realised that it's all just a series of pretty lights.

Do you worry about the characters in a movie once the credits have rolled? Do you feel angry at them? Do you feel guilty about going to the toilet in the middle of a love scene?

No, of course you don't.

In the same way, those of us who see the world as an illusion don't worry, feel angry or feel guilty about the characters in the "real world" movie - including the character of "me". Knowing it's all an illusion, just a bunch of atoms bouncing around, we can smile, let go, and let the pretty lights do whatever they have to do (which is obey the laws of physics). How can you be angry at atoms? How can you worry about what the atoms might do tomorrow? It wouldn't be rational.

This isn't all just some kind of idealistic philosophy. This is how some of us actually live.

Without guilt.

Without anxiety.

Without stress.

How can you feel angry at a bunch of atoms just bouncing around obeying the laws of physics?

Why would you feel guilty when you realise that is all you are?

If you just accept this is all nothing more than atoms, and enjoy the picture show, you will experience what I like to call permanent serenity - being happy with whatever is happening.

From Atman To The Universe.

According to recent measurements, scientific evidence, and observations, the universe appeared about 13.7 billion years ago. All of the matter and energy that exists in the universe today was there, in some form, in the beginning. This is known in physics as "The First Law of Thermodynamics". The law states that in a closed system (such as the entire universe), energy can be transformed, i.e. changed from one form to another, but cannot be created nor destroyed. Einstein demonstrated that mass (matter) and energy are the same thing, so this also applies to matter.

If, as we've discovered so far in this book, we now realise that what we are is an ever-changing conglomeration of atoms, all obeying the laws of physics, then the thing that is in control - the thing that we really *are,* the only thing left - is the universe, the "single, holistic continuum", consisting of atoms, sub-atomic particles, energy, dark matter and dark energy.

The universe is - for all human intents and purposes - eternal. The universe constructs all things and "knows" all things. It is omniscient. It is all-powerful.

The universe is the eternal, omniscient, all-powerful foundation of all things. It is "the One".

This all-powerful force was called other names by various cultures over the last few millennia, including:

- Atman
- Yahweh
- Brahman
- Buddha
- Allah
- Noumenon
- Consciousness

During more primitive eras of human thought, before the emergence of the modern scientific method, many philosophers and gurus had the insight that underneath the perceivable level of the world there must be something else, something that makes the perceptible level work. And they attached these names to it. As it turns out, their intuition was correct. However, where they sometimes attributed this force to a divine entity, today we understand that the force obeys the natural laws, the laws of physics and chemistry.

There is no need to attribute any kinds of anthropomorphic (i.e. human-like) qualities to this 'force'. Atoms don't have emotions or desires. They don't reward you for being good or for obeying scriptures and they don't punish you for not believing in them.

Atoms operate according to natural principles, which we refer to as 'laws'. In science, laws are fundamental principles confirmed and broadly agreed upon through the process of inductive reasoning. Of course, we don't claim to understand (yet) all of the laws by which the universe operates. We can be very confident, however, that it operates according to fundamental principles. Everywhere we turn our microscopes, telescopes and colliders, we see the basic matter of the universe operating according to repeatable principles, so it seems rational to assume that the better our tools become, the more laws we will discover and the more we will refine our existing understanding of the laws we have already discovered.

The only purpose that atoms serve is to fulfil their function. The purpose of a hydrogen atom is to function as a hydrogen atom. It has no special destiny, no dreams, no fears. It merely functions.

As you are made up of atoms, each serving its function, your sole purpose, too, is to function according to the nature and position of the atoms that make up your body at any particular time.

There is just one universe (that we are concerned with anyway). *You are that universe*. This is the "oneness", the "totality of all things" that the ancients referred to.

The separation we see in the universe, the duality of me and you, of atoms, is a virtue of our senses and our mind. Our senses evolved over hundreds of thousands of years to perceive macro objects. They aren't subtle enough to perceive the micro world, I.e. molecules, atoms, quarks, etc. So they do not perceive the full truth.

Our brains have evolved to make sense of what our senses perceive. Therefore even when we strip away the veil of the senses to discover the micro world, we still think of it in terms of separate particles.

Imagine for a moment that you were reduced by a shrink-ray down to a size smaller than a human cell. Imagine you found yourself inside a human hand cell. You sat and watched all of the cellular machinery doing their jobs. Wouldn't it look like a world of it's own? Each part of the cell might even seem to have free will or a level of intelligence, performing difficult tasks that all seem to be interconnected.

Then you start to slowly grow to full size again. As you grow larger than the cell, you start to see that all of the cellular mechanisms are just part of an integrated whole - the cell.

As you continue to grow larger, you begin to understand that the cells themselves are just a part of a larger entity - the hand.

The hand itself is part of the integrated body.

You continue to grow. The human body is part of the Earth.

The Earth is part of the Solar System.

Which is part of the galaxy.

Which is part of the Universe.

Imagine you were large enough to view the entire universe is one glance. And intelligent enough to perceive all of the functioning components of the universe.

Would it look to you like the cell? All of the parts operating together?

CONCLUSION.

Well, there you have it. Let's recap the basic Three Illusions.

1. You do not have free will. Every thought, decision and action is entirely determined by the laws of physics. Nobody else has free will either.

2. Time does not flow. Everything that has ever happened or ever will happen is happening right now.

3. You are not a unified body. You are an ever-changing temporary configuration of cells and atoms, a probability wave smeared out across all of space and time. There is no such thing as "you". You are the universe.

Once you fully comprehend these principles and integrate them into your thinking, I assure you that you will also experience the benefits I have mentioned. Greater peace with yourself and the world. Much less anxiety. Much less anger. Much less fear. You will find yourself living in the 'now moment' naturally and being content with whatever happens in your life. You will have happenness.

I challenge you to think deeply about these ideas and to tell me what you think. I'm always interested in hearing different perspectives and insights. You can contact me on email (cameronreilly@gmail.com), Twitter (cameronreilly) or Skype (cameronreilly).

May you have permanent serenity.

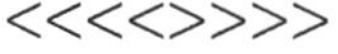

www.ingramcontent.com/pod-product-compliance
Ingram Content Group UK Ltd.
Pitfield, Milton Keynes, MK11 3LW, UK
UKHW041918190726
13854UKWH00003B/1320

9 781471 016981